Chickens

by
JOY PALMER

HODDER AND STOUGHTON
LONDON   SYDNEY   AUCKLAND   TORONTO

Note to the reader
The words in italics are explained in the glossary on page 30

The Author's and Publishers' thanks are due to the following for permission to reproduce photographs:

r = right; l = left; t = top; b = bottom

Barnaby's Picture Library: 13, 16, 12t, 23b; British Egg Information Service: 28; Colorific, Phillip Hason: cover; Chris Fairclough Colour Library: 24, 27, 29l, 29r; Holt Studios Ltd: 10; Oxford Scientific Films Ltd: 8, 9, 18; Pictor International, London: 4, 7, 17; John Twinning: 6r, 6l, 14 (SAPPA Chicks), 15 (SAPPA Chicks), 22, 23t; ZEFA Picture Library (UK Ltd): 21t, 21b, 21r

Artist: Ann Baum
Designed by Andrew Shoolbred
Bibliography compiled by Peter Bone
Picture research by Angela Anderson

The Author would like to thank the Association of Agriculture for its help and advice.

British Library Cataloguing in Publication Data
Palmer, Joy
    Chickens.
    1. Livestock. Chickens – For children
    I. Title   II. Series
    636.5
    ISBN 0-340-49924-9

First published 1989

Published by Hodder and Stoughton Children's Books, a division of Hodder and Stoughton Ltd, Mill Road, Dunton Green, Sevenoaks, Kent TN13 2YA

Photoset by Litho Link Ltd, Welshpool, Powys

Printed in Belgium by Proost International Book Production

Contents

page

Introduction   4

Breeds   6

Behaviour   8

Food   10

Free-range chickens   12

Deep litter houses   14

Battery farming   16

Enemies   18

Chicks   20

Eggs or meat   22

The meat we eat   24

The eggs we eat   26

Activities   28

Glossary   30

Bibliography   31

Index   32

Introduction

Chickens come in a variety of colours, shapes and sizes, although they are all members of the bird family. They have plump, *warm-blooded* bodies covered in soft feathers and, like other birds, they lay eggs. *Fertilised eggs* develop into baby chicks outside the body of the mother. Unfertilised eggs are important to humans as a source of food.

Hens and cockerels

A female chicken is called a *hen*. A male is called a *cockerel,* or cock. A cockerel is usually bigger than a hen, and has more

A Rhode Island Red cockerel and hens. The cockerel has brightly coloured feathers and is larger than the hens. ▼

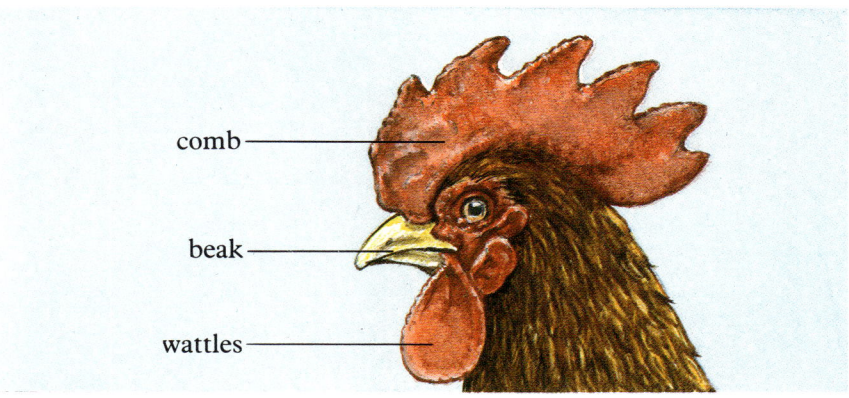

brightly coloured feathers. Both male and female have a small head, with a very strong, sharp beak for pecking grain and other seeds. There are bare patches of skin around the eyes. Hanging from the throat are two flaps of loose red skin called *wattles*. On top of the head is a *comb* – a ridge of red skin that stands up like a crown. The wattles and comb of a cockerel are usually larger and more brightly coloured than those of a hen.

A chicken's legs. ▶

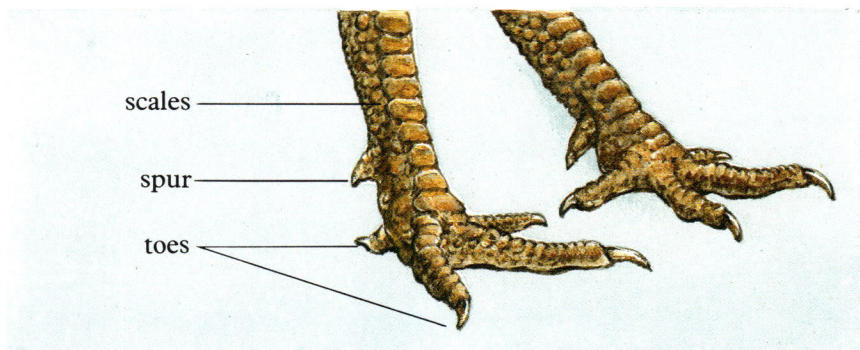

An adult chicken's legs are very strong, and are covered with scales. Its feet are also strong, in order to support its weight. Most chickens have four toes with sharp claws. These are useful for scratching on the ground for food, gripping tree branches or perching in a chicken house. Cockerels have an extra *spur* (or spike) which sticks out from the back of each leg.

A chicken's wings are rather short. As a result, chickens can only fly short distances. They rarely fly more than a few metres up to a perching place.

A chicken's tail points upwards and outwards. The cockerel's tail is much larger than the hen's tail. He has long, curved, arching tail feathers which are often very colourful.

Breeds

There are many different kinds, or *breeds*, of chicken. Most breeds on modern farms are related to the Red Jungle Fowl, the first breed ever known. Thousands of years ago, Jungle Fowl lived wild in the forests of South-East Asia. Then local people began to tame, or *domesticate* them and kept them for their meat and eggs.

Over the centuries, Jungle Fowl were bred and taken to other countries. More and more birds were reared, and today there are over a hundred different breeds of chicken throughout the world. Some breeds have been developed because they are attractive to look at; others because of the number of eggs they lay or the amount of meat they have on them.

Meat or eggs

Some big, heavy breeds, such as the Dorking or Indian Game Fowl, do not lay many eggs, yet they do have a lot of meat on

▲ The Indian Game Fowl is a plump breed of chicken, reared for its meat.

Exotic breeds with beautiful feathers are often displayed at agricultural shows. This is a Yokahama chicken.▶

▲ White Leghorn chickens can produce up to three hundred eggs a year.

them. Other breeds, such as the White Leghorn, are much smaller and lighter. They lay large numbers of eggs, one bird often producing about two hundred and fifty a year.

Some breeds both give good meat and lay lots of eggs. Farmers rear these breeds by 'crossing' two different breeds, that is, mating a *hen* from one breed with a *cockerel* from another. Their chicks are then *hybrids*, a mixture of two breeds. One of the best known hybrids is a cross between a White Leghorn hen and a Rhode Island Red cockerel. This bird lays many eggs each year and is also a good source of meat.

Behaviour

When a *cockerel* wants to mate with a *hen*, he shows off his colourful body by proudly strutting around, ruffling up his feathers and cleaning them with his beak. This is called a courtship display.

People who keep only a small flock of chickens usually have just have one cockerel. This is because cockerels are very jealous of rivals. If two cockerels are kept together, they will often fight over the hens with their claws and spurs.

Chickens which are free to wander round a farmyard, find most of their food themselves. They scratch the ground, looking for insects and seeds. Sometimes they are agile enough to catch flying insects in mid-air.

Hygiene

Chickens are very clean creatures. They spend a lot of time cleaning and *preening* their feathers with their beaks. They also roll and flap around on the ground, giving themselves a dust bath in dry soil. This helps them to get rid of any fleas that might be living in the warmth and darkness of their feathers.

Chickens preen their feathers to keep them clean and tidy. This chicken is preening under her wing. ▼

▲ Chickens rub themselves in the dust to get rid of fleas which live among their feathers.

At night chickens like to rest above ground. In the wild they perch on the branches of trees. Many farmers put special perches in their hen houses so that the chickens can fly up and *roost* at night.

Pecking order

A flock of hens always has a leader, or boss. The bossiest hen in the flock threatens the others and may peck them until they do as she wants. The next bossiest hen then threatens all the other hens, except the leader. The third bossiest threatens all but the first two hens, and so on. In this way, every hen has her own place in the flock's pecking order. The poor hen which is last in the pecking order is picked on by all the others. She is usually the weakest of the flock, and gets less food than the rest.

Pecking order.▶

The chief hen pecks all the others.

This hen pecks those below it, but not the chief.

This hen pecks those below it, but not the two above.

Food

A farmyard chicken has a varied diet, which may include worms, insects, grubs, seeds, grass, and some green leaves and shoots of plants. It finds its food by scratching the ground, turning over the soil to hunt for insects and worms. It uses its sharp beak to tear grass and plants, and to peck at seeds.

However, a chicken has no teeth, and so cannot chew its food. The food is swallowed whole and then passed down the throat into a kind of bag or pouch called a *crop*. Here it is stored until it becomes softer. The harder bits of food then pass into a second bag, called the *gizzard*, where they are softened and ground up. The softened food can then be digested. The goodness it contains can be used by the chicken's body to keep it healthy.

Diet

Good food is important, not just to keep the birds healthy, but to produce the yolks of their eggs. In turn, the yolks of *fertilised eggs* help to feed the growing *embryos*. Farmers must give the chickens extra food for a good and healthy diet. This may be the seeds of wheat or maize plants. It may be a

The farmer has to fill the food trays for the young chicks regularly.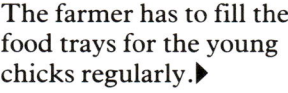

Some chickens are fed on corn to give their meat a special flavour. This diet turns their skins yellow.▶

Chicken food.▼

worm   insect

seeds   grass

crumbs   pellets

grit   water

specially prepared meal of 'crumbs' or 'pellets', made up of soya, cereals such as wheat and maize, fish-meal, and animal protein. Sometimes these ingredients are ground into a coarse powder called mash (concentrated feed). Food scientists are now looking into the safety of some of these feeds.

Free-range chickens may be fed kitchen scraps, such as bits of stale bread, vegetables and bacon rind. Green foods such as grass and leafy vegetables give them extra vitamins and minerals. All this food helps the birds grow strong and become good egg-layers. But if too much food is given, their diet may become unbalanced and their egg-laying reduced.

Grit and water
Farmyard chickens also eat grit (little bits of stone). The grit is good for them in two ways: it helps to grind and break up the food in the gizzard, and it also helps strengthen the shells of their eggs.

All chickens need plenty of fresh drinking water. They need water to live and to help form their eggs. In fact, two-thirds of any egg is made up of water.

Free-range chickens

Not all chickens have the same sort of home or way of life. By far the most natural way of keeping chickens is to let them roam freely during the daytime outside, where they will find food themselves. This food includes grass, insects, grubs and worms pulled from the ground. Some people think this is a more natural, healthy way of life, although it depends on how well the birds are cared for. Birds kept in this way are called free-range.

Free-range chickens spend a large part of each day outside.▶

Inside a free-range hen house.▶

perch

nesting box

At night, the farmer will put the free-range birds in a safe, clean house so that they can perch and be protected from cold weather and enemies. They will also be given some extra food such as grain and mash.

Many years ago, people often kept a few *hens* for eggs and meat in this way. Some people still do so today. Others run a *smallholding* – a small farm with just enough land to keep a few animals, and perhaps grow some vegetables and fruits.

Free-range eggs

Some smallholdings have enough hens to lay eggs for sale to the general public. When travelling through the countryside it is often possible to see a sign advertising 'Free-Range Eggs For Sale'. These eggs have been laid by hens reared on a free-range system. Shops which sell eggs must only describe them as 'free-range' if they have been laid by hens who are kept in this way.

Oddly enough, the egg-laying of free-range hens is affected by the amount of daylight they have. They lay more eggs in the summer when the days are longer.

Signs advertising free-range eggs can often be seen in the countryside.▼

Deep litter houses

Modern *poultry* farms, on which large numbers of chickens are reared, have to be highly organised. Many farms, particularly those raising *broilers,* young chickens for meat, adopted the deep litter system of housing.

With this system hundreds, or even thousands of chickens, are kept in one house. They stay there all through their lives and never go outside. The house itself is like a large shed without any windows.

The floor of a deep litter house is made of concrete. The farmer covers it with a deep layer of straw or wood shavings. At night, the chickens perch on wooden slats which have gaps between them. Their droppings fall through the gaps on to the floor of the house, which may be separated off from the birds.

Looking after the birds
Food and water for the birds is put into special containers called troughs or hoppers. The food is specially prepared and contains a mixture of soya, cereals such as wheat and maize, fish-meal, animal protein, and certain vitamins and minerals.

This photograph inside a deep litter house was taken with special lighting so the chickens were not disturbed. ▼

nest boxes

slatted boards

food
hopper

water trough

▲ A deep litter house is often noisy and smelly because so many birds are kept together.

A deep litter house may become very noisy and smelly because so many birds are kept in such a small space. If they are very crowded, the *hens* may get cross and peck at each other. This could also happen in a free-range house if the birds were crowded together. Sometimes a farmer trims the tips of their beaks so that they cannot hurt each other.

Whether they are keeping chickens for eggs or for meat, the farmers must make sure that the house is cleaned and disinfected regularly. If they do not, there is a risk of diseases spreading among the birds.

The food troughs must be kept very clean and filled regularly.▶

Battery houses

Most eggs on sale nowadays come from very large poultry farms. Some farms may keep up to a hundred thousand *hens* or more. In many ways they are more like egg factories than farms.

The hens are kept in battery cages. Three, four or five hens live together in a wire cage measuring about 50 cms square. The cages are stacked in rows. The hens spend all their lives in the battery house, which is lit entirely by electric light. Like deep litter chickens, they never go outside or even leave their cage. However, these houses are usually clean, warm and airy.

Feeding and egg laying

Food and water for the battery hens is put into troughs in front of the wire cages. This is often done by machine. The birds can put their heads through the front of the cage to reach the mash and the water.

Battery hens live in small cages all their lives. The battery house is lit by electric light so the hens never see daylight.▶

▲ Hundreds of thousands of chickens are kept in each battery house.

▲ Battery cages have tilted wire floors so that when eggs are laid, they roll down into a tray for collection.

The hens lay their eggs on the floor of their cages. The floors slope gently forward, so that the eggs roll down into special trays from where the farmer collects them. The hens' droppings fall through the floor of the cages on to the ground so that they can be cleaned away.

A good or a bad idea?

Many people think that battery farming is a good idea. They say that the hens are always warm and clean. They have a good, regular supply of food, and are safe from their natural enemies. Also, people want to buy eggs cheaply, so the farmer has to supply them at a low cost. Battery farming is a way of keeping a large number of hens, so that many eggs are produced at a low cost.

Others think that it is very cruel to keep hens in this way. They are crowded together, unable to move freely. Battery hens can become very bored and may peck and even injure each other if the sharp tips of their beaks are not trimmed.

Battery farming is not a natural way of life for hens because they cannot go outside. However, millions of birds are kept in this way. Many farmers are not happy with this system and are trying to find better ways of keeping chickens.

Enemies

Farmers who keep free-range chickens must take special care to protect them from wild animals hungry for food. These animals are known as predators.

One such predator is the fox. Foxes are very crafty. They can squeeze through very small holes in a fence or even tunnel underneath it. Unless free-range *hens* are safely locked up in a hen house at night, a fox may attack and kill a whole flock, even if it does not eat them all.

Other predators include badgers, weasels, stoats, rats and some large birds. Baby chicks are much more at risk from attack by these animals than are adult chickens.

Rats and mice are real pests near a chicken house. They are attracted by the birds' food. They can kill young chicks and steal eggs from the hens' nests. Rats can burrow under fences and chew their way through wood. Great care has to be taken to keep them away.

Hen houses are secured against enemies with wire.▼

fox

badger

weasel

stoat

rat

dog

cat

sparrowhawk

(Not to scale)

▲ These animals are natural enemies of the chicken.

Parasites live among the feathers of chickens. They can spread disease.▼

flea

mite   louse

Farmyard enemies

Unprotected chickens may also be attacked by farm animals, such as dogs and cats. Even if the danger is not great, chickens are generally nervous birds who often panic and give up the fight rather than try to defend themselves. Again, young chicks are more likely to be killed than adult hens and *cockerels*.

Disease

Battery farmed birds are usually safe from attack by wild animals. But, like free-range birds, they do run the risk of catching diseases. If one chicken becomes ill, the disease quickly spreads to all the other birds in the house. This is why *poultry* farmers must make sure that their chicken houses are cleaned and disinfected regularly.

Farmers also try to keep their birds free from pests, such as fleas, lice and mites. These insects are called *parasites*. They thrive in the warmth and darkness of a chicken's skin and feathers. Parasites can spread diseases, so chemicals called insecticides may be used to kill them.

19

Chicks

A *hen* lays eggs for most of her life. She normally lays one egg a day, although there are times when she stops laying. These times become more frequent as the hen grows older. Most eggs are laid in her first year. Eggs which have been fertilised may develop into baby chicks.

An egg is fertilised after a hen and a *cockerel* have mated. During mating, the hen squats down on the ground and the cockerel climbs on top of her. Their bodies meet and the cockerel's *sperm* pass into the hen through an opening called a *vent*. The sperm travel inside the hen to where her egg is growing, and the egg is then fertilised. When the egg is laid, it may grow into a chick.

The broody hen

After an egg has been fertilised and laid, the young chick takes twenty-one days to develop. During this time the egg must be kept warm and moist. The mother hen, often called a broody hen, likes to make her nest in a warm, dark place. Here she will gather her eggs until she has a dozen or so.

After an egg is fertilised the embryo grows for three weeks and then the egg will hatch. ▼

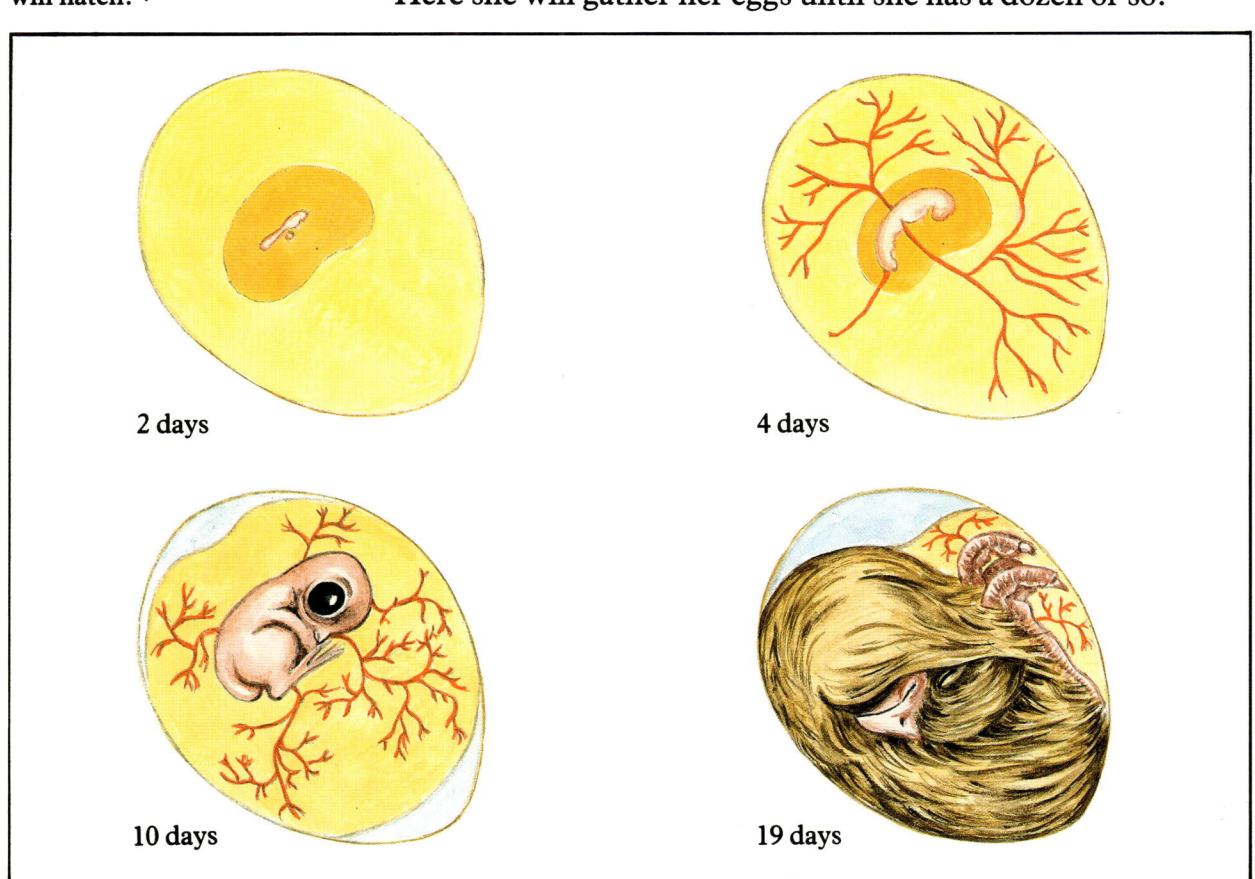

2 days

4 days

10 days

19 days

Then she will sit on the *fertilised eggs* to keep them warm and to help the chicks to grow. She ruffles up her feathers so that the heat of her body reaches the eggs. She also turns over the eggs from time to time, so that they are warmed evenly. Natural dampness from the hen's body provides the moisture that the eggs need. The process of helping fertilised eggs to grow into chicks is called *incubation*.

The growing embryo

While the unborn chick is developing in the egg, it is called an *embryo*. The embryo begins as a tiny white spot on the yolk, where the egg has been fertilised. Within a few days the head, body and tail of the baby bird begin to develop and blood is formed. After only three days, the embryo has a heart which pumps blood to all parts of the body. The chick grows steadily. Bones are formed, and skin and feathers begin to develop. The embryo is nourished by food carried in blood vessels from the yolk and white of the egg. There is just enough to keep it alive until it is ready to hatch on the twenty-first day. After exactly three weeks of incubation, the chick's beak is ready for the task of breaking the eggshell.

On day 21 the chick's beak is strong enough to break the egg shell. Hatching usually takes a couple of hours but it may be longer if the chick is weak.▼

Eggs or meat

Nowadays, a *poultry* farmer usually rears young chicks for meat, or sells *hens'* eggs for people to eat. If he or she chooses to rear chicks, the hens must first mate with a *cockerel* so that the eggs are fertile.

Eggs are only laid by female birds. A young hen starts laying eggs when she is about six months old, and continues to do so for most of her life. She will lay eggs even if she does not mate with a cockerel. More eggs are laid in the first year than in any other. Modern *breeds* of hen lay about two hundred and fifty eggs a year.

Incubating eggs

On large farms, where chicks are reared to be sold, the hens do not *incubate* their own eggs. Machines called incubators do this for them, keeping the eggs warm and moist for twenty-one days, and turning them regularly. Large incubators can hold thousands of eggs at a time while the *embryos* develop and hatch.

Incubating machines keep the eggs warm and moist. The trays tilt so the eggs roll over and are evenly warmed. ▼

Newly hatched chicks are kept in warm brooding pens. They stay here for up to six weeks.▶

Rearing chicks

Newly hatched chicks are housed in a brooding pen or shed where they can be kept warm. Unless reared by a mother hen, the chicks are not allowed outside until they are four to six weeks old.

Young female chicks are called *pullets*. They are normally kept for egg-laying. Young cockerels may be kept for breeding, but are more often reared for meat. In this case, they are given a good rich diet until they are between six and seven weeks old, when they are killed.

Pullets are young female chicks, reared for egg laying.▶

The meat we eat

Most chickens, whether free-range, deep litter, or battery, are eventually killed for people to eat. Some farmers rear birds called *broilers* just for their meat. When the broilers are six to seven weeks old, their meat is tender and good to eat.

Poultry farmers give the broilers food which helps to fatten them up quickly. *Feed additives,* such as minerals and antibiotics, are often included in this food. Most farmers use these very carefully, but even so, some people think that many of the additives should not be used at all. They say that if humans eat such chickens, they may also eat the additives, and these could be bad for their health. However, other people argue that the amount of additives given to chickens is so small that it does not harm the meat we eat.

Hen birds are also eaten, but a little later in their lives. Hens are most useful for laying eggs, especially during their first year. They lay fewer eggs in their second year, and even

The chicken meat in pies is usually from older hens who have spent most of their lives laying eggs.▶

24

fewer in their third. Most battery farmers keep hens for eighteen months or so, and then replace them with new young layers. The older birds are killed for chicken meat. The killing is done by specially trained people, so that the chickens are not in any pain when they die. Much of this meat is sent to factories, where it is made into pies and other products.

Many animals, including humans, eat chicken. The chicken eats animals smaller than itself as well as grains and plants. ▼

(Not to scale)

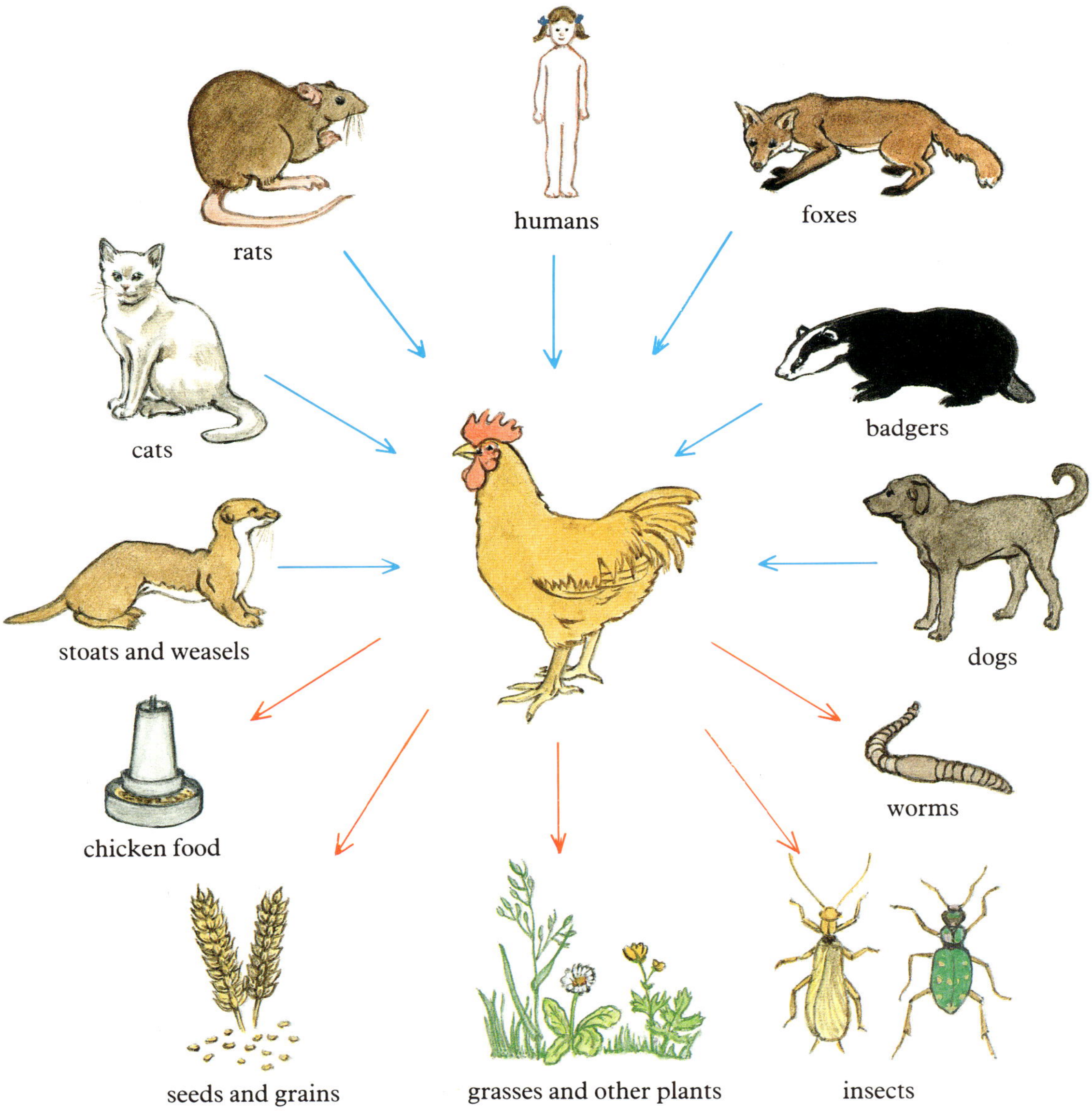

rats

humans

foxes

cats

badgers

stoats and weasels

dogs

chicken food

worms

seeds and grains

grasses and other plants

insects

The eggs we eat

It takes about a day for one egg to develop inside the body of a *hen*. Egg cells are formed in the *ovary*, and each egg cell has a yolk. Every day, one of these egg cells leaves the ovary. It travels down a tube called an oviduct. This is where the white of the egg forms around the yolk. Next, a thick skin (or membrane) grows round the yolk and white. Last of all, the eggshell is made. The completed egg leaves the hen's body through an opening called the *vent*.

A healthy food

Eggs are a rich source of food. They can keep an *embryo* alive for twenty-one days. They are also a good food for humans, though it is important to cook them well to kill any harmful bacteria. Eggs are full of proteins, fat, vitamins and minerals. These minerals include calcium, iron, magnesium, sodium, copper, potassium, sulphur, phosphorus and chlorine. The vitamins include vitamins A, B, D and E. An egg can give humans enough energy to last for several hours. This is why many people like to eat eggs for breakfast.

Every day an egg leaves the hen's ovary and travels down the oviduct. It leaves the hen's body through the vent. ▼

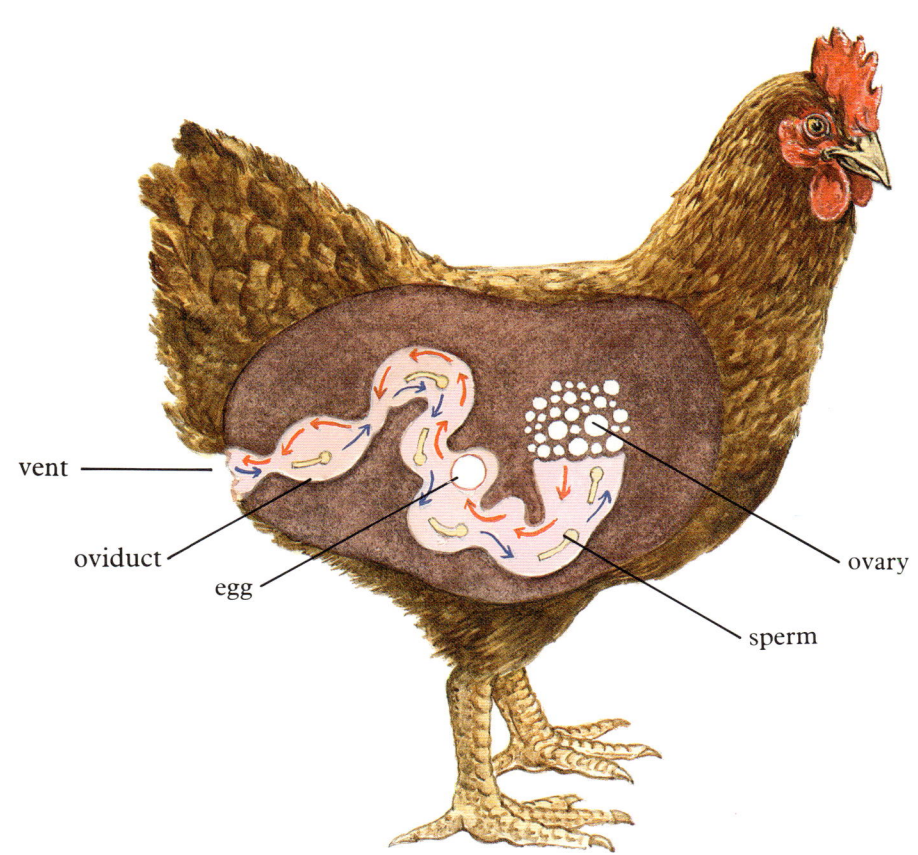

vent

oviduct

egg

sperm

ovary

Eggs are a rich source of food because they contain proteins, fat, vitamins and minerals.▶

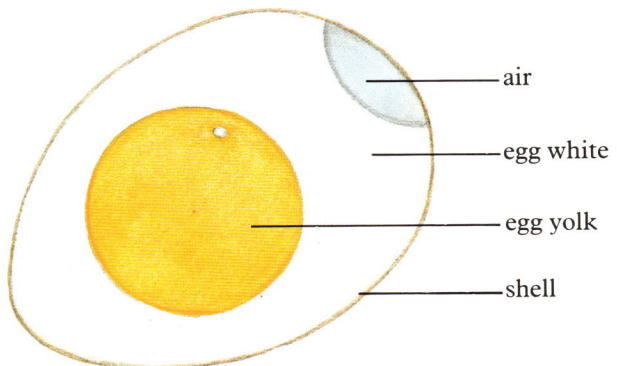

air
egg white
egg yolk
shell

However, some health experts believe that more than two or three eggs a week are bad for you. This is because they contain cholesterol. If we have too much cholesterol in our bodies we are likely to develop heart disease.

Some people believe that free-range eggs have a better flavour than those which come from a battery house. This is probably a matter of personal choice, although it is very likely that free-range hens have a more varied diet, and this may affect the taste of their eggs.

Free-range eggs and battery eggs look the same, but many people believe they taste different.▶

Activities

Decorating eggs

Hundreds of years ago, the Chinese used to paint or dye eggs to celebrate the coming of spring each year. Today, eggs are often decorated at Easter.

How to do it

Eggs to be painted or decorated must first be hard-boiled or 'blown' (emptied). To blow a raw egg, make a tiny hole at both ends of the shell with a needle. Next make the holes a little larger with a skewer. If the skewer is pushed carefully into the egg, it will break the yolk. If you then put a basin underneath the egg, and blow through one of the holes, the yolk and white will gradually run out. Be patient! It can be a long job. The empty egg can then be painted or decorated with pieces of material, felt, glitter, paper, seeds, beads – or anything else you can think of. Remember – an empty eggshell is very delicate. It must be handled very carefully.

These eggs have been blown and decorated to celebrate Easter. ▼

Recipe: Ham and egg under a blanket

Warning: Cooking can be dangerous. Ask an adult to help you prepare this dish.

For one person you will need
1 egg
1 slice of bread
a little butter
1 slice of ham
a little grated cheese

Cook the egg by placing it in an egg poacher or by cracking it into a little hot water for about six minutes.

Toast the bread and then butter it. Put the slice of ham on the toast, and warm it under the grill or in the oven.

When the egg is cooked, place it on the ham. Sprinkle the grated cheese over the ham and the egg.

Put everything back in the oven or under the grill until the cheese has melted.

To make *Ham and egg under a blanket* the egg is first poached and then baked with the other ingredients. ▼

Glossary

Breed A type or variety of bird or animal.

Broiler A chicken raised for meat.

Cockerel A male chicken.

Comb Red, fleshy crown of skin on the head of a hen or cockerel.

Crop A bag or pouch into which food passes from the throat.

Domesticated Tamed and reared by people.

Embryo An unborn chick inside a hen's egg.

Feed additives Substances mixed into an animal's feed to make the animal grow faster.

Fertilised eggs Eggs laid by hens who have mated with cockerels. A fertilised egg can develop into a chick.

Gizzard A second bag or sac into which food passes from the hen's crop, and where it is ground up.

Hen A female chicken.

Hybrid A variety of bird produced by mating or crossing different breeds.

Incubation Helping chicks to grow by keeping fertilised eggs warm and moist for 21 days.

Ovary Part of the hen's body in which egg cells are formed.

Parasite A small animal or plant living in or upon another.

Poultry Birds kept for eggs and meat, including chickens, geese, ducks and turkeys.

Preening Cleaning feathers with the beak.

Pullet A young female chicken.

Roost Sleeping or resting at night-time, usually on a perch.

Smallholding A small farm where people keep a few animals, and perhaps grow vegetables and other crops.

Sperm Sex cells from the male body.

Spur A spike at the back of a cockerel's legs, sometimes used for fighting.

Vent Opening under the tail of a bird. Sperm pass from male to female through the vent, and waste passes out of the body this way too.

Warm-blooded A creature whose blood maintains a steady, warm temperature.

Wattles Loose flesh hanging from both sides of a chicken's face.

Bibliography

If you want to find out more about chickens the following books may be of interest. Your local library should be able to get copies for you.

Back, Christine and Olesen, Jens.
CHICKEN AND EGG.
A. & C. Black, 1984.   0713624256

A pictorial book with excellent "cut away" views of different stages in the egg's development.

Burton, Jane.
CHESTER THE CHICK.
Purnell, 1988.   0361078544

Chester the chick is seen from the moment he emerges from his shell and we follow him through the first year of his life. Excellent photographs.

Coldrey, Jennifer.
THE CHICKEN ON THE FARM.
Methuen, 1987.   0416638708

This book considers free-range hens in particular.

Nature's Way.
THE CHICKEN AND THE EGG.
G. Whizzard/Andre Deutsch, 1979.   0233970568
Lavishly illustrated book with a separate, and detailed text.

Whitlock, Ralph.
POULTRY.
Wayland, 1982.   0853409366

A more detailed look at the life cycle of a free-range hen. There is a useful section on commercial incubators.

Peter Bone
Senior Librarian
Children's and Schools Services, Hampshire County Library

Index

battery house 16-17
breeds 6-7, 22, 30
broilers 14, 24, 30
broody hen 20-21

cockerel 4, 7, 8, 19, 20, 22, 30
comb 5, 30
courtship display 8
crop 10, 30

deep litter house 14-15, 16
diseases 15, 19

embryo 20-21, 30
enemies, natural 18-19

feeding chickens 10-11, 12-13, 14, 16, 25
fertilisation 20, 26
food chain 25
free-range 12-13

gizzard 10, 30
grit 11

hen 4, 7, 8, 9, 15, 16, 17, 18, 20, 21, 22, 24, 26
hybrids 7, 30

incubation 21, 22, 30

laying eggs 11, 13, 16, 17, 20, 21, 22, 24, 26

mash 11, 13
meat 6, 7, 11, 14, 22, 23, 24, 25
minerals 14, 26

ovary 26, 30

parasites 19, 30
pecking order 9
pests 19
predators 18-19
proteins 26-27
pullets 23, 30

roost 9, 30

spur 5, 30

vitamins 26-27

wattles 5, 30

yolk 21, 26, 27, 28

PRINTED IN BELGIUM BY

INTERNATIONAL BOOK PRODUCTION